THE MAN WHO SPOKE TO THE BIRDS

FRANCK BOIVERT

Copyright © 2023 Franck Boivert

All rights reserved.

ISBN:

Contents

The Man Who Spoke to the Birds 1
The Strongest Man in the World 5
The Man Passing through a Wall 12
Christmas in Tonga 17
A Moment of Joy Shared by Two Men 23
Kaneka Rugby 28
Tears in Heaven 33
The Big Game 42
Sundays in Lézignan 53
Play with Your Heart 57
Manon 62
Barefeet 64
Philosophy with Waisale Serevi 67
Fiji Olympic Champion 78
The Last Men, the Real Ones 84
Pichou 91
Afterword 95
About the Author 99

The Man Who Spoke to the Birds

We are in the St John's Marist club, Suva; the capital of Fiji, the moist heat was sticking everywhere.

This is after training; I am sitting in an armchair that I enjoy a lot after the runs in the darkness.

We started by playing touch, and then the night arrived very quickly.

When we could not see the ball fly from hand to hand any longer, we all gather at the end of ground. The coach is Pio Tikoisuva the only Fijian who had the honor to play with the Barbarians back then and the captain for the Fiji team who beat the British Lions. He speaks quietly in Fijian. It is a pretty long monologue. When he is done I ask the player standing next to me who is no other than Aliposo Waqaliti the captain for Fiji 7's who won several times the prestigious Hong Kong tournament and he answers simply with a very low voice, that we are going to run.

In the darkness then we ran, long sprints, shorts sprints, sit-ups, push up, jumps. Pio in between two exhausting exercises spoke again, calmly without raising his voice in spite of the fast debit of Fijian words. Aliposo would lean against me and in an even lower voice would say: " we are going to sprint to the end of the ground, come back at full speed and go again". Useless to say that I was arriving last one in these sprints and the darkness of the night could not hide me. But my teammates respected me still and sometimes I was beating the props.

Now it's over and I can enjoy a Fiji bitter in a tiny glass that my hosts fill up with delight.

At the end of the table, two of them say nothing, busy around the kava that they prepare in a big wooden recipient called Tanoa or kava bowl.

The club president is sitting there, beside me and chain-smokes his cigarettes. On the other side of the lower table is Father Wilson. He is waiting impatiently for the first kava bowl. We start the conversation, the Kava finally arrives, I swallow it, and I sit deeper in my armchair. Father Wilson swallows his, the three clap in their hands to punctuate the drinking of the assembly members. The punctuations are not as firm as the ones I get to receive.

The priest is a regular of the place; he is the principal of the Marist school and a fervent supporter of the Rugby team.

He carries on the conversation and then he makes a connection between my nationality and the one of the priest he is to tell me the story.

He Father Wilson is Irish, but this priest is French, from Normandy. He arrives in the Fiji Islands and he is sent to evangelize an isolated village where no one has even dared to go.

You had to have a damned courage to push inside the forest following the river. At the time you could still find Maccabees hanging on the trees following the human sacrifices to whom Fijian were forced into following their beliefs. They were may be also the victims of some tribal war who were cut short as soon as there were some casualty.

But that did not stop at all the French priest.

He reached the village, how no one really knows. What we know is that the village adopted him.

What we know is that the priest not only evangelized the village but also became an extraordinary personality in the village. The villagers adored him, he brought a joy, a peace who were transformed in a prosperity that the village had never known before, not only a material prosperity but also spiritual.

The village knew a harmony and became a true Eden, all this thanks to the teaching and the fabulous personality of the priest who came from Normandy.

The end of the human sacrifices, source of stress and formidable tensions for this small society must have played a crucial role. But there must have been much more than that. Many astonishing events took place thanks to his persuasion and the goodness of this man.

This man was not ordinary, he also spoke to the birds, and he was their friend just like he was everyone's friend in the village.

Sometimes he had to be absent to come and visit the diocese in Suva.

The birds would come along with him and accompany him till the edge of the forest. Then the father would turn towards them and would tell them to wait for him, that he would come back. And the birds would go back but were all there to welcome him upon his return.

Extraordinary things, we said it, happened there in this village during all these years. The father consigned everything on his register. He wrote down a lot, told everything, his emotions, the births, the weddings, the events the soothed dramas by the serenity and the strength the villagers had found.

But all these fabulous things, we will never know about it.

One day, one very sad day, he received a letter from the archdiocese. He was to be posted in another village and had to leave that Fijian village to which he gave so much love.

Mad with pain and sadness. He stacked all of his writings. His registers, and his souvenirs and burnt everything, and he had to go...

Father Williams takes his bowl to his lips for a little more kava. My legs feel like cotton, my exhausted body was floating in the clubhouse air, Not sure if it's the effect of the Kava or the Fiji Bitter.

I just know that Father Wilson has finished telling us the story about the French Father who came from Normandy and spoke to the birds.

Suva 1985

The Strongest Man in the World

He was back from Seattle, there the season starts much earlier than in Southern California.

They don't play there, starting end of November until the rain and the snow stop falling down, early March.

That year I find him with a broken ankle and he won't be able to start the season with us as it starts early November here in Southern California. It is not playing that his ankle got broken; it is, he says during a fight in a bar, yes around Seattle…

He tells me about the fight for which he is not responsible at all, in fact it is not the fight he tells me about, but more how he broke his ankle.

He is really sorry. He is probably the strongest man in the world. He is even the man the strongest in the World.

As a matter of fact this is what affirms Bill, another player, lawyer by trade, who has bound more than once his body to Chris's in the scrum let it be behind him as second row or binding in the front row.

I respect this opinion; the scrum is the only place in the world where one can really judge a man's strength.

Bill that night in the pub was going from one to another and was asking everything in every one: who is the strongest man in the world? Of course as coach of the team my opinion was determining. But Bill knows the answer; or rather he wanted to tell us.

I could think of our other prop, Randy a Samoan square built, thick, indestructible, only muscle from calves to the shoulders and neck. And he has a large frank smile that cannot stop laughing. I feel really comfortable next to him, you know nothing is going to happen to you in that pub, he reassures with his calm, his good mood and his kindness. I know he adores me especially since the day where I taught him that you drink red wine with meat and white wine with fish. Each time I see him he talks about it and confirms that when he will go to France, he will make sure to order red wine with meat and white wine with fish…

I don't think Randy went to France or will go one day but I would love to host him in my country and take an immense pleasure to see him order his wine at the restaurant.

But Randy is not the strongest man in the world, it's Bill who says it, he is the second strongest man in the world. We must believe Bill not only because he rubbed his ears in the scrum with Randy but mainly because Bill is a guy always joyous and optimistic.

So we only can agree with him.

Bill did the Vietnam War, he still wears at times his old military uniform, the famous 101 airborne with the eagle head crest on the upper sleeve or a cap that he wears proudly and amused. He has two Amerasian little boys that we all adore when he brings them to the game in his old convertible triumph. He had told me how he ran his first marathon in Vietnam; the US army had pacified the 42,195 km of the road just for the runners. The GIs were posted all along the course barrel bayonet and machine gun nests every 500 meters and a squadron of helicopters flying over.

With all this deployment says Bill; I better finish that damned marathon.

Bill is now a lawyer in one of these big firms located in the Downtown LA skyscrapers. He does not communicate any longer by onomatopoeia with his partners; something he was doing all these years in Vietnam in the middle of the jungle and of the fear, he could just talk this limited and obscure language that only the soldiers of his platoon could understand. Bill is in his forties now but he will always play his rugby, he has too much Scottish descent he says.

The strongest man in the world then, is well liked by his teammates however he is not expansive. He is as generous as he can especially for those who respect him and that he likes.

He is one of these American workers completely independent, a contractual. His specialty is to lift transformers on the electrical posts.

One says he is so strong that he can lift the transformer by himself on top of the post. When his contract is finished, he looks for another job; he could stay sometimes weeks without any work.

He is single, we don't know any girl friend of his, and he lives with his mother but often in his pick-up truck. He does not pay taxes, no social charges; he is paid cash and earns much more that way. And he is free!

But at times his face is inundated with sadness and you can feel an inner anger. I guess his frustrations in the southern California rugby.

He did not get any selection, the blonde ones from the rich universities selected among themselves. They did not consider the ones not out of their elitist fraternities.

But on that day in Las Vegas, we got them all right!

We made to the final of the tournament. It is true that our players from the "Valley" had less money to lose all night long in the immense casinos.

Our players may be, slept more than the others...

As usual the morning of the final of the tournament we were counting first the injured before we could select the team and announce it to the team. There were way too many to brave our Los Angeles rivals, those who live and practice not far from the beautiful beaches. Those can attract the rich graduates of UCLA, USC or Berkeley. Those who can invite the #8 for the Argentina Pumas to play for them or this New Zealand star or the prop from the National team.

But in a final, on one game, we know that the rough ones from the Valley can match them. So I prepare them and organize them accordingly. I can feel in their attitudes, their confidence that this time they can win. Ok so everything looks good especially Chris who played thunderous elimination games the scrum squashed all of its rivals. One day an old New Zealander told me that you build your team around the tight head prop. The tight head prop, its Chris the strongest man in the world. I build the team around him. Everything falls into place. My guys will be valiant, I am sure of that but about anticipation in the game I cant find one today who is not daredevil enough to take care of the defensive coverage of the kicking game of this New Zealander 10 and this English 15 who are going to play behind and around us all afternoon with their smart kicking game.

Ok so I take advantage of so many injuries to explain them I select myself at flanker

I am lucky those who don't play are absolutely broken and don't grumble.

The selection is announced in a hotel room too small for 20 huge guys. But when calling each name I remind them their role in our strategy that we put in place.

But when I call Nolan, who has a crucial role in our plan that is to stop that English 15 who comes into the line on all of their plays, no Nolan in the room! But I can hear his Northridge accent in the bathroom where I find him all naked in the bathtub trying to relax his hamstring, in the warm water, Nolan is a bowl of muscles forged in the magma of American football, I go over his role in the bathtub, he is still butt naked!

The game starts and of course it is the grand combat that we promised ourselves.

Nolan on the first ball touched by the 15 dismantles him and that 15 is going to spend the rest of the afternoon way deep in his position.

Brian is our hooker and nothing scares him. Before the game, he is worried about me, he has a hard time to see me his little French coach in the middle of this fracas of immense bodies that spent their youth to weightlift for the titanic shocks of American football.

For Brian this is his environment, this is where he has fun with his massive bulldog body and his daredevil temper, he thrives in the explosive tackles, the shocks from hell and the aggressiveness at its climax.

Brian does not come often to training because he has to work hard as the manager of a rental car agency. I rent from him often a Cadillac for the price of a small sedan. In Las Vegas he wants to gift me one of these beautiful women and he does not understand that I accept the Cadillac but not the beautiful women who are not as expensive.

I reassure Brian, I will still be alive after the game, yes he tells me because he will be there to protect me. Brian indeed I can count on him prodigy of American football, he had won a scholarship for Nebraska university who at the time was the strongest football team in the country. But it was too cold for Brian in Nebraska, so he let down the scholarship and American football, all of this in spite of his extraordinary malice and his outstanding athletic talent for the games of combat and ball.

Brian will always be there in the trenches in this final just like all of the 13 other players who charge anything that moves and comes from the fancy Los Angeles neighborhoods the fifteen's one it's me, the trenches I go there when I cannot do otherwise, however I queen the pawn to this 10 and this 15, I manage to be each time where they try to place the ball to make us go backward. But all of this I can do thanks to Chris. In the scrum I just rest my shoulder on him, no need to push behind him, he destroys his opposite; he is the boss, the main beam. It is the rock that makes our whole pack go forward. Their halfbacks are under pressure and their kicking game is even more miserable. In the rucks, Chris is a monster when he gets in them; he is like a bulldozer that clears everything on its passage and our pack follows, enraged.

Of course we win this game, this final, this tournament and when come the time of the awards, they have no choice but give it to Chris as best player. A prop best player! MVP!!!

What a great revenge for Chris, but when I spoke to him about his fabulous game and his award, he took it with modesty, with humility, saying that he was awarded mainly more for his longevity than for his rugby prowess in that final. I disagreed with him and I know he was really pleased even if he did not say it and never will.

I am not really sure where about is Chris now.

A friend told me that he was not doing too well lately. His retraining as a coach did not go very well.

You can't be a coach and be bitter against all. He became almost paranoid says the friend and always carries a gun now (is it because he does not feel as strong any longer?) and just like too many white people of the Californian working class, he started to dislike Mexicans, scapegoats of their disappointments and frustrations.

It is a shame he was the strongest man in the world…

Las Vegas 1981

Franck Boivert

The Man Passing through a Wall

Like a lot of rugby stories, it has to start in a New Zealand Pub thousand of miles from our subject.

But still this is how I understood everything about my favorite game. In order to understand everything, it took thousands of miles and then some months stuck in between a couple of years.

But this does not matter at the moment, as the empty glasses pile up on the bar, the foam still stuck on the glass walls. Then more pitches arrive real brown, well covered by the white and cool collar.

This is the ideal moment to please your self, my companions talk rugby of course, and it just takes one easy maneuver to have them recall the French players. Now that the beer has liberated them, they jump onto the legends, and among them they go back to these famous players from the 1968 tour.

That's it! Here we go! This one positions himself in the middle of the pub room, the circle steps aside, he takes three steps back, tries to look light, relaxed, loose. To keep his balance he holds his glass half full, at arms length, he lifts his nose up just a bit.

Then he recreates this run up like others recreate traditional dances celebrating the eternity of the legends. The run short and relaxed ends with nice movement of the leg kicking an invisible ball. Since there is not a ball on the wooden floor, our goal kicker with his free hand shows the imaginary flight that ends up by a straight signal, the ball went through the goal post like a straight arrow.

He turns towards the eyes brightened of excitement and admiration. Yes he passed the penalty goal from 55 m in the corner, there was mud, and there was wind, cold! , It was in Wellington. He reminds to me the laughing and teasing when the French fullback told the referee that he was going for goal from 55 m in the corner! With the mud, with the wind, the cold! Step away I show you again and here he goes again, the look well straight; we are witnessing the umpteenth repetition in a new Zealand pub of Pierre Villepreux goal in the second test All Black-France in Wellington in1968.

But my enjoyment is not going to stop there, in the indulgence of the beer and the easy friendliness of the pub. I have them tell me about the legend Jo Maso.

Just like all my generation's players I admired him and nothing in the pub now can stop the adjectives in the group of drinkers who just gets bigger and bigger. It is a one up-manship that beats the beer rounds flat seams. Each and everyone add his appreciation and unanimity is reached around each dithyrambic expression. A true athlete, magic, extraordinary, you name it…

But the essential, the image for the memory, it is this attitude, this pose they all recreate, here with the beer glass in place of the ball. The head high, the bust straight, they try to imitate that class, this incomparable beauty, and the aestheticism that no one could think of finding in a rugby stadium

So of course I laugh, I enjoy totally. Almost tickling my belly like a big baby who gets his favorite feeding bottle.

Dreaming in a New Zealand pub about legends, reassures you on life's values, it is a real pleasure.

It is also a pleasure to see the others still dream and share their dream. They dream of the impossible, of the surreal. They dream of a man who was passing through a wall.

" Jo, this is the way they call you over there, "the man who was passing through a wall"

We are now very far away from Auckland or Christchurch. Birds squeal in the cypress and the sun floods the red of the clay tennis courts.

I tell Jo about my stay in the southern hemisphere, but when I evoke to him this man who was passing through a wall and who was no other than he, he turns his head modestly down, but straightens it up by passion for what he is about to explain me.

No in fact it was not that hard to go through the All Blacks defense.

I explain you. Time stops, the tennis balls come to a rest, the birds keep mum in the cypress, the friends can wait, and I am about to hear a revelation.

A revelation for me, because in a few instants I am going to understand the magic, the extraordinary and how you make men dream.

Before we listen to Jo, lets go back to 1968, when the France team plays the third test in Auckland. This test I discovered it thanks to a Denis Lalanne article in "l'équipe" the sports newspaper. This article written years after this game had been played wanted to explain the advantage of a fly half who attacks, and Denis Lalanne was lamenting rightly so, these fly halves which only talent was to have monumental kicks. So as a counter example he tells about the game Jo played as a fly half of the French backline in this third test in Auckland, Denis Lalanne, assures us that France should have won that game if it had not been for imaginary forward passes seen by the local referee, because in these times, the referees were the ones from the host nation and not neutral. But this is not this point. What is of interest it is the extraordinary game that JO played lightning the French backline.

For our New Zealand friends who still dream in their pubs, they do not understand. Their defense, it was a wall. It was a wall because they had a back row also legendary.

Kirkpatrick, Tremain and Brian Lochore.

Such a back row cannot be beaten in defense!

Especially by a fly half!

No, no, assures calmly Jo.

They had one flanker who was coming up full pace on me. So that one I was waiting for him and I was standing deep enough and since he was coming up full pace, just a small inside cut was beating him.

The other flanker I did not have to worry about him because he rushed in second curtain towards our wing, so as he was not looking after me I was beating him in his back. After my inside cut I accelerated full on so I could take the gap between their fly half and their number eight to whom I was escaping by maintaining my acceleration.

That's how a man goes through a wall

New Zealand 1985

USAP tennis club 1986

Christmas in Tonga

In the hustle of Nuku'alofa airport, he stands straight, the pale light of the tiny arrival terminal barely lights his blonde and white hair and his "hello Franck Welcome to Tonga" resounds over the buzzing of the crowd.

It was just before Christmas and the Hawaii airlines Boeing was packed to the rim of Tongans and Samoans who were bringing back in their luggage for their Christmas with the family, television sets, radios, refrigerator, washing machines, video cassette players from the USA.

At the stopover in Honolulu, the pilot announces on the speaker as we were already rolling on the tarmac that we had to return to the terminal as the plane was overloaded and could not take off, I look around me and I am squeezed in between an immense Samoan lady and a huge Tongan gentleman, both of them on their lava lava in honor of their return to their country. Delay then for Hawaii airlines that had to get rid of several luggage in order to be able to take off.

But all of this does not seem to surprise Jerry, who is now the manager of the airport bar, an airport which luggage delivery hall is no bigger than our garage at home, there are piled up suitcases, packages, bags and you have to climb on these heaps to finally find your luggage who luckily did not stay in the plane for its next stop, Apia, Samoa. All of this, with the help Tongan men and women, in a jovial mood.

I met Jerry first in Southern California, he was a referee, and he was indeed an excellent referee and our favorite one, always in a good mood, confident, he would blow the whistle only for the basic faults. He had the respect from the players; I really enjoyed him...more over he had the talent to say a gentle joke in between a ruck and a scrum.

In the line out he would ask for the tunnel to be straight "keep it straight! Oh yes this is what she told me also last time…"

For Rugby Magazine, he had spoken about the hell in Vietnam that he had survived. He was so grateful for his fate and his life that he promised to himself that after the Vietnam War, each day should be like a Christmas day.

I remind him this sentence on Christmas day that we spend together in Tonga.

He answers "yes I try to tell myself that its every day Christmas for me, but too often its tough"; referring himself to the post traumatic war syndrome of the war veterans.

Even tougher that he just won a battle against a cancer with a vitamin regime, workouts and a will to fight it.

He runs each day on Tongatapu with his beautiful spouse from Taiwan and her magnificent strong legs.

They swim together till Atata the islet in front of Nuku'alofa.

Jerry tells me also about his experience with the Tongan rugby team during the very first rugby world cup in 1987.

May be you have seen him during the games of the men with the red jersey. He was manager, physiotherapist and fitness trainer…

He still pesters against the selectors who felt obligated to play in the first game, the Prince of Tonga who had not played rugby for years and had not done the fitness preparation…and was way too old to participate in a World Cup.

But that was the Prince, and his nobility overruling, he played the first game versus Canada.

Game lost, but Jerry swears they would have won without the Prince thanks to his fitness program taken out of the Seals commando method. The elite commando unit specialized in sabotages, on or behind enemy coastlines.

So Jerry has his Tongan players to run, jump, crawl, climb. The Tongan players are not too inclined to hard effort. Life is sweet in Tonga…

During one practice, the players exhausted complain that all these work outs, really hurt.

Jerry then turns into a rage, yells at them that they don't know what hurting really means, and to demonstrate them what hurting really means, he lights a cigarette and sticks it on the back of his hand. As the ash burns his skin, he screams at the players, do you know what hurts? This hurts! It hurts a lot, but I can take it!!!

The Tongan players look at Jerry totally stupefied.

They will be tonic, and in great shape during that world cup and will cause all sorts of problems to the Welsh, the Irish and the Canadians.

Jerry however has a lot of respect for his players, he can see them during lunch break, jump over the stadium fence, catch a chicken, and they do a fire in a corner and roast the chicken that way.

He remembers also that player who separated his shoulder during a Sunday game at the world cup. Jerry goes to support him and carry him out. The player is in tears, "you cry because you hurt" enquires Jerry?"

No answers the player.

"I cry because the Lord punishes me for playing on a Sunday."

In Jerry's simple and comfortable home, there is hanging on his office wall the knife he used during his commando days in Vietnam.

He points towards it and says without any emotion: this knife killed seventeen people.

He lets himself convince to tell us some episodes that he actually wrote down in a book.

His greatest fright was during a night ambush near a river at night. All senses awaken, and the finger on the trigger of his machine gun, he watches over the enemy. But he realizes that someone else is watching him over. Hidden in the darkness, is a huge tiger. If Jerry shoots at the tiger, the whole operation fails and he endangers all of his men in hide out. The enemy is so close. The tiger is even closer. It is an untenable position. After a silent face to face, the tiger withdraws and disappears in the darkness.

During another operation, his commando leaves the submarine to swim towards the enemy coastline. As he goes up towards the surface, he notices an unusual activity at the water surface. He finds himself in the middle of thousands of sea snakes gathering for their reproduction period. They are extremely aggressive during that time. Their numbers is incalculable on a thickness of several meters under the water.

Through radio he alerts his men to go back to the submarine, mission is aborted.

A reconnaissance plane sent on the zone will discover several hundred square meters of sea snakes.

Several times he barely escaped death, especially the day his helicopter crashed in Vietnam, he managed to get away with it with just some broken bones, almost the same, says he that when he was a rodeo rider and he credits his experience as a rodeo rider in the Midwest for surviving the crash.

I never saw Jerry again after my passage in Tonga.

A Tongan friend has told me that he was in Hawaii for a visit in a military hospital.

The other day one told me that he was now battling yet another cancer in an Arizona Hospital.

Jerry, where are you? Let's put on our mask and snorkel and let's go swim in the lagoon towards Atata. The multicolored fishes will look at us surprised, and then we will drink one of your Budweiser beers you used to import, under the coconut trees. The orange sun will paint the evening colors on an outrigger canoe that passes by.

We will remember our rugby memories from San Diego to Christchurch from Tongatapu to Monterey.

It will be Christmas in Tonga

Nuku'alofa 1988

A Moment of Joy Shared by Two Men

Elliott looks up towards the sky in this morning of a young November, the grey clouds are stronger, autumn comes back suddenly, just like each year.

On that weekend the fall will not celebrate the Celtic festival with a sky still blue and warm of an Indian summer.

It is ok, his woolen kilt will be lighter to wear, even if it will less sparkle with its reds and greens, in the grayness of the rain that hesitates in becoming the first snow.

Brian's eyelids are kind of heavy still and fatigued from the cheating lights of Reno's Casinos.

He spent there too many hours in the depth of the night trying to do like everyone else. Play vanishing dollars captivating him with dreams of extravagant gains.

He was not dupe though; he knew he lost his concentration at a key moment in the game. This beautiful waitress, with her long legs and her low cut that he could not ignore, he wanted to take a look at her for yet another lost dream in his solitary fantasies.

Yes this charming waitress took his whisky order, just when he thought he had guessed the mystery of the playing cards dancing in front of his eyes. But it does not matter, she smiled at him, she neared her beautiful round boobs that he could glimpse only. A furtive moment of happiness, beauty, in the middle of this swarming of games and players slouched in front of their slot machines and the tables of cards and roulettes.

He did stand out of this mediocrity that softly suffocated him by wearing his Celtic suit. His beret with the two proud feathers planted was giving him nobility that no one could claim in the place.

A place where men and women are just hunted beasts by the lure of a lucky and lazy gain. Bodies all curled up and hypnotized by the silly numbers and signs.

In the cold night he met again the loneliness of a Celt from Scotland in the immensity of the Sierra Nevada. The bright and blinking lights never changed his melancholic soul and tough at the same time that he had forged on the ranch.

The ranch where he had smothered his youth, there in between two mountains, one wooden and one bared by the winds, the snow and the lights of the hot summer sun.

But still, he had his bagpipe which complaints had the fallow deers cry and even the eagles in the valley.

Come the night he has the echo of his hoarse and vain songs vibrate.

He wears again his beautiful ceremonial costume, his long woolen socks, his clan's jacket and the kilt tartan.

He is going to join all those, who like him do not want to forget where they come from going to a country with no costumes and where you are afraid to get lost.

In the morning he goes to the Celtic festival. He will find there the dancers, the musicians, the storytellers, and the drinkers.

He will watch the Highland games, the stone put, the caber throw.

But this time around, a surprise was in the program.

At eleven am, the local university plays a rugby game, a game he has not seen since his departure from the ancestral land.

He smiles as he looks at these American students clumsy and naïve passing with no elegance this marvelous thing that is a rugby ball!

Elliott is hesitant at meeting them, to show them how to share with more elegance the oval.

On the other side of the ground, the other team warms up, better organized and more confident than the Nevada beginners.

He meets again the acquaintances that stroll in between the highland games, the tents under which are sheltered traditional souvenirs but also the barbecues with the roasted meats smells.

But Elliott cannot keep his eyes away from the green rectangle. He waits impatiently for the kickoff of the rugby game between Stanford University rugby team and the one of Nevada Reno.

He can feel the pre-game excitement, the apparent joy of the locals to fight it out with the Californian students who travelled several hours by bus and even crossed the Donner Pass in spite of the first snowstorm of the year.

All those who go by tell him about it and repeat it, but they don't stay for the game. There is too much to do, the barbecues, the dances, the games...

Elliott shudders on the first tackle, he stretches on the first hit of the scrum engagement, he raises on his toes on the first attack in passes that fails extremis, he slightly twists on the clearing kick from the fly half.

His body, his eyes, his head vibrate on each action.

The images of rucks, mauls and counter attacks mix up with the one he had almost forgotten.

He can see again the white lights that surrounded the rugby field somewhere around Berwick in the heart of the Scottish borders. His nostrils remind him the smell of the wet thick grass of Scotland, his muscles the joy of running, tackling, wrestling.

The young Americans don't know really how to manage to score a try, but all of the sudden the Stanford wing makes a break, jukes a defender with an outside cut and then accelerates irresistibly to score right under the goal posts Elliott claps his hands, his eyes brighten with happiness and nostalgia, he remembers this last try he scored by swinging his hips to beat the Melrose fullback on the outside and finish sliding under the goal posts the ball passionately held two hands on it so the ecstasy does not go by too fast.

He recalls the hot teas in the warm baths after the games. He remembers Mary ginger smile and of the heart she had drawn in the foam of a Arran that he no longer dared to drink and the Van Morrison music in the pub's warm evening.

The game is over, he had resisted to the desire to enter the ground and play, he too. He thinks he can still do it. He goes to the young wing who scored the try and tells him enthusiastically "well played young man". The Stanford student looks at Elliott's tired face, a face lit by a furtive happiness. The Celt lost in the Nevada Sierra Mountains gets in return a luminous smile from the young wing.

A moment of joy shared by two men.

Reno, Nevada 1995

Kaneka Rugby

From the speedway, the only one on the island, we saw the small stage lit by the colored light spots. So we took a right turn and we went to check it out.

The football ground, this is where was organized a small music concert. A few stands were selling barbeques and drinks.

Bands were taking turns on the stage, they all played reggae and some local music, a kind of soft rock music.

Some young Melanesians were dancing in front of the stage. We saw about two or three Europeans only.

A band from the neighborhood steps on the stage and try to sing "Rosie" the famous Francis Cabrel song. They are beginners, it's cute, but clumsy and it makes the girls next to us giggle, as they know the lyrics better than the singer himself.

Sure, Cabrel is the most popular music for the young Kanak. Cabrel and Reggae music are the one music Melanesians really love.

Then comes on the stage a Wallisian band who plays nice Polynesian melodies, I adore Polynesian music, so present in the South Pacific.

But the dancers disappear and the musicians play in front of an empty space.

I cannot believe such disrespect for such a cool music. Did the organizers anticipate this and were they expecting this sort of boycott?

I understand quickly the situation, especially when the next Melanesian band steps up on the stage and dancers and spectators are back as well.

When I landed at the airport, I could not ignore the French soldiers behind the sandbags. I know what has happened here, and I learn quickly what occurred between these communities during what the locals here call "the events".

These Wallisian musicians are really tranquil on the stage with their guitars, but it is Wallisians who were beating up the Kanak "Independantistes", not so long ago in the Noumea Streets. It's the Europeans who had their guns pointed towards these very same Melanesians; it is the independantist Melanesians who trapped when they could Europeans and Wallisians.

But on that night here is this kanak band that with on top of the electric guitars and drums bring up the traditional music percussion instruments, they try with their traditional beat to create their own music, their own Reggae.

A couple of years later I am back, the sandbags are gone from the airport and with them the soldiers.

Kanak music followed its destiny and the Kanak bands have integrated their traditional music instruments, finally is born a modern local music, it is the Kaneka.

You cannot ignore the beat of these songs that even the French Radio RFO plays. You got to be really uptight not to dance on Kaneka music.

That year my colleague and friend Fenan asks if I would be interested to look after this Noumea suburb neighborhood where he tries to launch rugby as an activity.

He warns me that in this neighborhood not many Europeans dare to step foot on it, but that everything should be all right especially for me, and my independantist Catalan and Occitan accent.

It is only after a couple of sessions that I realize that this ground on which I coach rugby to the young Melanesian, I know it. It is the ground where was this music festival.

Fenan was right

All the neighborhood kids adopt me and me too I adopt them but I have to adapt my coaching. Out of the question to set up organized structured practices like it would be done in the USA or New Zealand.

So it's playing that is the priority, playing for playing to have fun, to enjoy, to feast. Sure there is no thoroughness in defense, (who cares!), sure there are some rugby fundamentals who are not respected (who gives a damn!).

But I have a blast! I have a blast watching the "Montravel kids".

The ball is never buried, it flies from hands to hands, the player does not charge head down in the bunch of the defense, he is looking for the pass, if possible the most improbable pass that will leave stunned the defender…and the coach. I marvel of the dummies, body dummies, scissors dummies, kicking dummies, one-handed dummy and of course simple dummy passes who send the defenders the wrong way.

On Saturdays, we have to play against the Wallisian kids, they are strong and powerful and from the chicks (9 years old) to the Cadets (14 years old), we are kind of scared when we step on the field. So the ball we have it circulate even faster the runs have all sorts of angles. We never get caught with the ball, it works, well sometimes it does not, and we argue that our rugby men play bare feet, as they cannot afford to buy boots or even running shoes. But we win almost each time. And most of all, it may sound egoistic but this is my favorite style of play that I witness on the sideline. A fun rugby, joyous, full of pace like the Kaneka, it is the Kaneka rugby.

Just like a kid at night I fall asleep dreaming the Kaneka Rugby wins the Hong Kong tournament just like the Fijians did. Or even that we design a XV kaneka rugby that would spin the head to all these brutal teams who can see in Rugby just a mean to satisfy their superiority complex.

Now at my demand in the tournaments, the young rugby men bring their drumsticks and in between two games the beat comes up from under the shade of a tree or from a spot in the stands.

The whistle blows and here comes the oval ball taking the beat of the kaneka. The ball sings, laughs, has fun, the ball has a big smile that crosses her face full of lights. The players call her, caress her, brush her, and have her vibrate just like the bamboo drums. She does crazy things take journeys she never dared to take, gets lost and finds herself in paths and meanders that renders her tipsy of life.

Just like the music we want to follow her pace, we want to immerse ourselves happily in the Kaneka Rugby. But watch out, you will have to keep the head high, hold the supreme jewel with your hands open, and be quick in the debauchery of creativity and inventions. You have mainly to accept the unpredictability of its madness and its delusions.

Then stoicism will lean towards humor and fall over in an uncontrollable giggling

If you are ready come and play Kaneka Rugby.

Nouméa 1991

Tears in Heaven

I had told them that I would come by to say good-bye. I am late because of a stupid disciplinary commission for which I had to write a report. The night has already fallen, a black night even if young. I leave the expressway towards Montravel. I am going to say good-bye to all my young players of this Noumea neighborhood, the place where we invented the Kaneka rugby.

Last Wednesday was our last training. A hell of a last training! Of course they arrived one by one, or two by two, nonchalant like if nothing exciting was going to happen on this ground.

However I know that I just need to put the ball in play and all of the sudden, the yellowed ground grass, becomes green of happiness, the clouds let the tired sunshine rays of a late afternoon brighten the place, birds squeal again, so excited in the hill bush. The Kaneka rugby is played again. The ball shoots in all directions for the tipsiness so anxiously awaited for. They run, they scissors, they loop, they fake, they double up, and they call the ball that they share willingly.

This is the training that I enjoy the most; I am more of a spectator than a coach. My role is just to reinforce what is beautiful, efficient, technical, exciting, amazing, funny, tactically well played and am enthusiastic.

But all of the sudden I stop the game; they are upset. The joy, the pleasure, the love for the game is interrupted.

So they listen, if I stopped, it means that something is really wrong, a mistake that I cannot forgive. I tell them, I explain them. The one who did it, tries to hide; the others disapprove and even jokingly make fun of him and he does not dare to correct his mistake…its okay.

Play is on again they all have eyes wide opened even the guilty one, ready for the super interception, or to the magic pass, or even the miracle pass. Sometimes I anticipate the game and there I encourage the scissors pass between Didier and Joel, the 2 brothers play it perfectly. Just at the right moment and I burst into admiration of such a perfect timing, so precise and accurate in front of a defense still so good…

I adore all my players but I have a soft spot for Joel.

However he is not as enthusiastic as the others and he is not close to me all the time, like the others are, they are all hungry for stories, advices, exchange, dialogue, listening. It is true that when they tell me about their young Kanak adventures in the changing world of the Noumea "cités". They find me quite attentive. Their sincerity, their candor, their naivety, their innocence amuses me, surprises me, has me be reconciled forever with life and human kind.

Joel, he is more independent, when I talk to him, he does not like to engage the conversation. His shyness will bring his hand behind his neck; the elbow up, he will hide his glance. I can guess that all he can think about is to flee this embarrassing moment.

Some days I can see him alone, on his bicycle, he rides along the harbor, his fishing rod, well stuck on his shoulder, he is looking for the spot where he can settle down waiting for the fish to bite. Other times I can see him busy above his bag or battling with his hook. I can see him happy with his blonde curly hair, his minuscule ponytail and his determined look.

When he plays rugby Joel has me dream. His hands are like magnets to catch the ball, his cuts in the run elude all of the defenders, his accelerations are thundering, his runs are beautiful, the head high, the ball caressed.

Joel is a rugby gem, Of course, he has absolutely no idea, and all he cares about is to score over there and to do it by having good fun.

He is small, so in defense he is going to hang on to the big attacker, he will manage somehow to bring to the ground the ball carrier, with no big hit but with a fierce determination.

I know effectively that Joel could be a fabulous three quarter of the land rugby; he is a little genius.

But let's leave him tranquil to his fishing, he is going to see the sun make bright white spots on the lagoon, the water is going to whisper songs and dreams that he, only, will hear, and may be tomorrow in the vibrant clamor of the play, he will stop his defender and with a goose step will overlap him irresistibly.

At this particular training, the ones with a white t-shirt were on that side, those with a colored t-shirt on the other…. I know in five minutes they will all be bare chested, but you got to start somewhere to make the teams! Today a little European is present, and I put him in Joel's team who does not want him:

"Not him Monsieur"

"But why do I ask him?"

"But he is white Monsieur!"

In my head things are racing. Gee, he is racist against the little white boy!

Nothing like racism to make me yell and be stern. But I can't manage to be that stern.

So I say to Joel: " Then help him, show him how to play, give him advices, help him".

Joel looks at me seeming surprised. He returns to his team, not so convinced, but he understood me, or I hope so.

Did Joel make a racist remark? Was he discriminating? Is Joel racist against the white kids?

If Joel had not been the kid I like so much, I believe I would have shouted, I would have punished him and forced him to apologize to the little boy.

Because I like Joel I had to make an effort of understanding to find out what this attitude meant and therefore give a pertinent answer.

Joel did not want a bad player in the team, because he wants to win. But the little white kids, frankly, they are not as smart as the little Kanak. These ones run, jump, climb the trees, play outside, as soon as they finished sleeping, eat or go to school.

The Europeans kids, they are more cocooned by their parents, spend more time in the car for the strolls, watch television, go out less because outside, its hazardous, there are spikes, holes, severe weather.

No. Little white kids cannot play good rugby, they can barely run, they have no agility, they are too lumpish.

This is what Joel was thinking when he said with disdain, "but he is a white", Monsieur.

So when I answered "then help him", I wanted to tell Joel: you, you are lucky, you are always outside, you run fast, your bare feet know where to plant themselves in the grass, or brush the burning stones.

Your shoulders know how to dodge branches and tackles, your senses know about speed and knocks.

So Joel it is not because he is white that he cannot taste the turmoil of the game and savor his body in motion.

Is it the good answer for Joel?

I hope.

If I had shouted, punished and asked Joel to apologize. Would he have learned the respect of the other?

But to fight this nascent prejudice, I was lucky to deal with a small chap that I liked.

If he had been a big asshole should I have done the same or should I have acted the same way?

I was thinking about all of that when leaving Montravel, then I took the Vallée du Tir, rather then the express way, I drove slowly to have a better look at the life of this lower class neighborhood, the car windows down let the odors of the Kava float then vanish in the purple twilight. The pale lights welcome the encounters, the ni-Vanuatu is going for a last minute shopping, the one from Mare comes out with bread, the one from Ouvea, speeds up the pace to buy one conserve, the Chinese tidy up his hardware store, and laughs break out in between two from Lifou and one from Kone.

The same laughs who have inundated of joy and happiness, the rugby ground just some moments ago.

The laughs of giggles, then two, then three girls play now with my encouragements and don't we have now Corrine who tackles and stop dead Jean Paul, nicknamed Poulain (Foal). This one is on the ground dumbfounded to have been tackled by a girl. And here we have them all burst into laughter, a beautiful laugh, irresistible of drollery and frankness.

We cannot stop that laugh, they roll on the ground of laughter, pass it on, pass it back, when it seems to go away, like the backwash of the wave, here it comes back sparkling on the four corners of the ground.

Once these laughs were bursting non-stop in the greyness of a delicate and sweet rain.

The grass was sliding under the soles of the bare feet, the foot work was getting lost and escaping and here we have our players falling down in the funniest of the positions, on the butt, on the belly, the chin in the flasks of fresh water.

Practice was interrupted for these parties of laughter we never got tired of.

How I hate this whistle, to end these fabulous rugby practices where the joy of the game had as only enemy, time. Fortunately, there is always a next time.

Except for this time. We push back the dark colors of the dying day, and then we can't play any more. I whistle one last time with a lumpy throat from emotion.

I leave again above the Pacific Ocean in a few days. And I am afraid forever.

I arrive for the good bye; it is the smallest ones who welcome me on the parking lot. Their shouts of joy guide me, as the lamppost is too tired to be able to distinguish my little friends, girls and boys. As usual, they flood me with questions, answers, and small stories. In the distance I can hear a very cool sound. That's it I know what are they preparing. In the depth of the darkness gets nearer the twitches of the Kanak beat. But the little ones, in the confusion, assail me; this one offers me a t-shirt, a small photo, a necklace of white shells.

I thank him but his answers are: it is Aquinin who gifts you this.

Then I can see little Aquinin who watches us from the distance but shy away as soon as I see him.

And that's how the whole evening is going to go by, they will cover me with t-shirts but the one who is offering it will always do it through one of their friend boy or girl.

The "juniors" and the "cadets" arrive finally. Their drumsticks and their bamboos drum percussions found their way after several halts to start again the beat and the approach.

It is the Pilou, all circle up, and they whistle or cry out to punctuate the four beats. Hips and feet get tangled.

The circle is around me and Joan the leader of the group declares that to thank me to have coached them, they were going to perform a Kaneka.

Sounds invade me from all sides, and Jean Marc and Lomu intone a song about the revolt of the young Kanak.

They all take hear and in unison with full lungs:

"Down with the colonial Justice!"

I can't believe it and I am not sure they realize the political meaning of the lyrics. Their performance is impressive of enthusiasm and conviction and the love of the music. They progress with other popular Kaneka songs, T-shirts and necklaces flow. Then each group performs a song, the girls, and the "benjamins", the "poussins" who are their rugby category.

The "Benjamins" sing a wonderful song in English with the guitar. I recognize the song but can't quite identify it, so I ask them; " it's Eric Clapton Monsieur, it is a song from Eric Clapton".

I recall now "tears in heaven"; the song Clapton composed after the tragic death of his 5 year old who fell accidently from the 30th floor of his building.

Here again, I am not sure they realize the depth of the lyrics in English.

"Would you know my name, if I saw you in heaven?"

And I answer when the song is over

"Yes I would!"

I have to go; one last Kaneka number and I climb in the car, loaded with necklaces and emotions.

When I take off they are still 3 or 4 to run after the car shouting good byes.

I come out of the parking lot and after the bend; I speed up for the straight line while wavering with the hand. It's then that the first of the line on each side of the road, passes a rugby ball to the next one placed a couple of meters away and this all along the street, the 2 balls go as fast as the car and form like two garlands. The ball passed they form right away a pack of shouts, good byes, laughs. In the rear mirror, I can see the arms that wave and the smiles that disappear. I found myself alone but on the passenger seat is a huge pile of t-shirts and necklaces that tinkle against each other at each bend.

My invaluable gifts!

> *"I must be strong*
> *And carry on*
> *Cause I know*
> *I don't belong*
> *Here in heaven"*

Noumea 1991

The Big Game

Twenty years after I wish I was with "my players"; 15 warriors who led us to the only win in the Big Game.

I remember the clear sky and the bright sunshine in this Northern California early March. I remember the grass, the trees and the hills of Strawberry Canyon, the shouts, the tears and the sweat of that day.

The game went as a movie that goes according to the script. I remember that like in all of the most important games I coached, the one you aimed for, the one you prepared for, the one you expected, I had no stress at all, no anxiety, I just felt calm and focused. An almost strange state of mind that would not correspond to the drama played on and around the field. I had that exact same feeling in the last World Cup final I coached and in the 1995 final, and other final games.

I guess it is because I felt I had done my part. After my part, it is the players who take over the game; it belongs to them.

We won this game not on that day but during the season and the seasons preceding it.

We were never as professional as Cal; we picked up players right before the season some times during the season. We could not plan any recruiting, we did not have players at Stanford just for rugby, we just went as things were coming our way, we just did not have the choice. All these seasons we were never supposed to win, some times not even close, however I always prepared that game to win and I was always convinced that we had a chance to win. I knew there was a way to win in each game and believed it so much that all these losses year after year hurt me and I would come away always upset after the losses.

It changed in this final of 1995. Before that final I had one of my best speech ever. I recall it had to do with all the dictators around the world who had been chopped down and that now it was our turn to chop down Cal outrageous dominance in USA Rugby. Again no one believed in our chances but supported our valiant effort. Especially when the opposition coach tried to destabilize us by having change our jerseys colors right before warm up but the Stanford student's sense of humor prevailed. This game we should have won but for an unlucky bounce and an injury to our star player and game breaker, it would have been the greatest ever. We played a huge Cal team stacked with Eagles and great players.

I recall before that 1995 final game being really worried about this Eagle center in particular; he was a real threat to our defense and could hurt our whole plan. This star player got totally shut down with the defensive organization we put in place and that had to do with Chris Grasso our center twice smaller than his opposite but Chris had a courage three times bigger. The team had terrific fighting spirit and kept its intelligence and determination throughout. An intelligence well illustrated in a line out where the opposition coach was screaming in our hooker ears to jump in front of our #2 Jumper Jeff Siemon an extraordinary athlete son a of a legendary American football player and our other Jeff (Freund) full of malice called for a throw as a lob that beat the Cal jumper and enraged the opposition coach. That day was may be the first time I felt so strongly these senses of almost detachment to the game like if no emotion could interfere with our concentration. Not even that scrum won against the head by our front row lead by flamboyant Brian Brennan. Looking back winning that scrum played on their own "22", right there in the middle looks as big of an achievement for our players as getting to the top of the Everest.

So here we are in this bright afternoon that all of Stanford Rugby was waiting for.

I do not recall if we had an overall game plan, I do not think so as we always practiced to play whatever is ahead of us. And so we did.

I recall very well the details that made the difference in the tactical preparation of the game.

For example Cal played a very tight slide defense that would shut down our main weapon, our fullback Bobby Blunt a devastating runner.

I looked for a solution and even consulted in the off-season Jo Maso the Great French center. He gave some good suggestions but finally I thought of asking our swift center Tim Yarnall to run with the slide by attacking the back of his sliding opposite number, and then extend his arms to pass wider to Bobby who would cut the slide with pace.

It worked on each of our backline attack and created disarray in Cal's defense all afternoon.

At the time rugby was still a very structured game for all teams. We did not want that. We wanted to be different and in our game there was no "taboo", we would take any opportunity. Perhaps the greatest moment in the game was when Cal was pounding our goal line and our defense made of solidarity and organization was holding these formidable players any way we could. Holding it so well that another massive tackle made of guts and courage forced a Cal player to spill the ball right on our goal line. One of our players recovered it and saw right away the left side totally open, the ball was quickly passed to Dave Warter our super fast wing who just ran from the end zone as all were expecting him to kick the ball away. He made it all the way to the 40 m Cal line crossing the 50m line after a beautiful "frame overlap" on a last defender. The Cal cover defense came to the rescue, but so did our support with Rj and also "Norm" and also Shervi. The crowd was screaming, and all Dave had to do was pass inside to the support for a 100 meters try. The stands were going crazy and being incredibly noisy; Dave did not hear and see all our support and just did not beat these last defenders on his own. It was still a stunning moment in the game, but at the time it looked so "natural" to us; on the sideline this was just what I expected.

Finally came the try, we were dominating and leading, but we needed a try to liberate the game.

It came from one of our classic phase well played and executed. In order to "fix" the very fit Cal back row, we needed to drive the lineout, and roll out the maul towards our backs before launching our backline. We had another line out on Cal's 22, we won it as we had fantastic jumpers with Jeff Siemon and Jeremy Toner helped by our "cleaner" Jeff Freund who had perfected a line out throw technique borrowed from the snappers of American football.

We excelled in that exercise of driving the maul and twist it just as the defenders started to regroup. After that phase the ball got spun swiftly by our scrum half Shin Inoue in such a way that Mike Weiner, our fly half, would get the ball already in motion for the "dummy one/two/5 in" specially designed for Bobby. Bobby came outside Tim all game long, he was not expected in the middle, the timing was diabolical, with rage he shredded the defense and went untouched flying in the end zone. Yes flying, before he scored he dived in the air. This dive seemed as it lasted an eternity, the eternity of heaven, when every thing come to a halt, when all your coaching life passes in front of your eyes, the practices in the cold, the rain, the joys of victories, the pain of injuries, the hours in front of the video, the bus trips, the drills you loved, the scrums you packed, the screams you shout at the 3.30pm practice, the red sunset on Maloney fields; all of it goes by, as Bobby flies in the air and then referee Don Reordan who lifts his arm and bends his knees to signal an historical try.

In our tactical organization I always wanted the best runner covering the kicks. That is why I always placed the best runner in the forwards at number 8. Jared Hopkins was just a phenomenal athlete with power, speed, determination and great intelligence. As I expected, at one point in the game he got the ball with plenty of space to use this outstanding running ability. A Cal wing kicked the ball away as he was faced by our line of defense, the kick landed right in the hands of Jared inside our 35 meters exactly where he was to be positioned. The game was deep in the second half and the players of both teams were a bit scattered around the field, exhausted by the intense and merciless battle. Jared saw some space towards his right, he beats one, 2 defenders and ends up running along the sideline with incredible speed and power. A defender comes across that he brushes aside, the goal line is only 5m away, one last defender comes across and throws himself at Jared's legs, he resists this last attempt, but loses his balance and as he does, extends his arm to place the ball on the goal line.

THAT'S IT, WE WON.

Or this is what we all thought. But with 4 minutes to go, our flanker Shervi hurt his ankle; he still packs this last scrum in the middle of the field. Kevin Dalzell the USA Eagle captain beats him easily as he takes off from the base of the scrum and Cal scores a very good try. Poor Shervi who had fought so bravely all game long. He was not supposed to play that game because in our team we had the most incredible open side flanker I ever coached: Trung Ngo. Trung got injured before the game; he is on clutches on the sideline. If he had played, our victory would have been more emphatic, he was standing at 1.75 cm may be, but had the energy to tackle mountains for 80 minutes. He would average 15 to 25 tackles a game, an incredible statistic for this level of play. He was an extraordinary player.

After that try from Cal, there was just enough time for the restart. And then something extraordinary happened. Both teams kept the ball in play for 3 minutes. For any technician of the game, this is an exceptional thing to happen. Very rarely does the ball stay in play for that long, even at the highest international level. Cal was desperate to come back and threw the ball and its energy left all over the field. Stanford put all it had in these last 3 minutes of continuous play. We turned the ball over a couple of times and still kept it in play. What a contrast with the current professional rugby players who kick the ball out of bounce or run in touch just to finish the game so unceremoniously. Not a chance with the Stanford players, they took the challenge of the game all the way, Cal would attack, and we counterattacked and played no matter the score, the moment in the game. Rugby life at Stanford is too short not to cherish every single second. For every single second we shall keep the ball alive, make it sing …and we play!

…With "panache".

This game would not have been that great without a great referee, one with class who called only 9 penalties in the whole game and let both teams play so positively especially for these last fantastic 3 minutes,

It is over; our fans made up mainly of the second and third team invade the pitch, crazy of joy and disbelief. Arnaud still has his horn that he blew all game long; Hubert is with his camera to immortalize the team of heroes. The picture taken does not have just 15 players, it has ALL the Stanford players, those of the second team and third team who had also their part in the victory, in the glory.

Before the game started, I had spotted a public telephone at this building in between the rugby stadium and the tennis courts. I did not take part in the immediate celebration, even missed the presentation of the axe. I slipped through to that building and away from the noise and the cheers I called Elise, the one I wanted to share my joy with the most. We ended up both crying on the phone, she was in New Caledonia.

I remember all our loyal friends being there, some are gone already, Ray Nielsen, Don Bunce and of course Emile Bruneau.

Tom Klein who had engineered from the start the rebirth of Stanford Rugby was walking all smiles among the players carrying his son on his back. Jason Bucha was there, Brian Brennan, Jennifer Chue, Francine, Sandy and others I should not forget.

In the bus taking us to the post game party, Jeff Siemon our captain reminded us to stay humble in victory and so we did indeed. I just recall on Highway 101 some strong happy singing. That was about it for the celebration and Ten Years After it is about it too.

Above my bed in Perpignan is pinned the grass I picked from Strawberry Canyon rugby field after the game, it is kept there, sealed in a plastic bag.

Today Saturday March 11, 2006, I am somewhere in the world wearing the Stanford "white crème" sweater (just like 10 years ago) to celebrate the Rugby players who had the virtue I learned to cherish the most: loyalty.

Front row: Sean Noonan, Jeff Freund, Joe Clayton
Locks: Scott Whitt, Jeremy Toner
Flankers: Jeff Siemon (captain), Shervi Malakzadeh
#8: Jared Hopkins
Scrum half: Shin Inoue
Fly half: Mike Weiner (rip 2001)
Centers: Chris Grasso, (replaced temporarily for blood bin by Nick Murat), Tim Yarnall
Wings: RJ Delee, Dave Warter
Fullback: Bobby Blunt

Stanford has never beaten again Cal in rugby that was the only win in 43 years.

Shervin Malekazadeh is now a professor of political Sciences at Colgate University and is often a consultant for CNN and other networks as a specialist on Iranian politics

Shin Inoue Founded and running a nonprofit, The Flagstone Initiative, to provide a financial shock absorber for low-income renters, improving financial stability and helping prevent eviction. Lives in New York

Dave Warter is vice president of E&J Gallo wineries. Lives in Modesto, California

Mike Weiner passed away from a heart attack in a swimming pool in Israel

Jeff Freund lives in Montana after multiple startup companies.

Rj Delee is a surgeon in Oregon

Jared Hopkins is the financial director for Michigan Medicine health services.

Joe Clayton lives on his farm in Idaho

Jeff Siemon is vice president for General Mills

Bobby Blunt currently works as divisional Vice president of Quality engineering for Abbot, Cardiac Rhythm management (CRM) in Sylmar Ca.

Tim Yarnall lives near Stanford and published a book on his father Dolan Cureloglu who was a celebrity in Turkey as a Psychologist.

Chris Grasso was a helicopter pilot for rescue missions in Iraq and Afghanistan.

Nicolas Murat is a business banker in Dubai.

Sundays in Lézignan

My grand mother's shop, Manou was located in Guynemer Street, and was facing a poultry shop as well as a flower shop.

This is where we came to meet again my cousins, my uncle who had his workshop at the back and of course my grand mother, the charcuterie was famous for its "saucisse" as customers would come from far apart to buy it. We would play under the iron work display tables pretending we were in a car, the shop closed at 1 pm and then came the time for lunch that we took in the adjacent dinner room. Lunch had four dishes, the hors d'oeuvre with ham, pate, and grated carrots and black blood sausage.

Then came the main dish, meat with assorted vegetables. Then the cheese, then the lettuce and finally the desserts with chocolate éclairs, apple pies and other patisseries as the coffee was served for the adults, we could see already in the street the crowd walking towards the stadium to watch the rugby league game with the famous Lézignan rugby league team, this was our team, the team my father and uncle had played for.

So once the coffee drank, my father and uncle would grab their jacket and off we go with my cousin Jean, to the stadium just like everyone else my father and uncle would wear their shirt and tie. My brother Denis and Pierre my other cousin not fan of rugby would stay back most of the time with my grand mother, my aunt Tantoune and of course my mother. So, all the men would walk to the "stade du Moulin" (windmill stadium), the Den of our team. On the way we would walk through the railroad crossing, then longed the vegetable gardens with my grand mother's one who were located behind the stadium grand stands, these were wooden made and we would sit on them after my uncle and dad would exchange some jokes with their old friends they had grown up with. All the spectators were of course dressed up, tie, shirt and three-piece suits. Among them we could see some first-world war veterans; some with the face purplish as they had been gassed, others without a leg and others that my father was pointing out to is with part of the skull gone. Of course all the Lézignan notability was there in the stands, the mayor, the main lawyer and the notary. They would follow without any excess the exploits of our heroes, Gilbert Benausse and his brother Rene and of course Andre Carrere who was playing fullback and would run back all the balls with so much pace. He had a cropped haircut that I had asked the hair dresser to do exactly the same on me same with my cousin Jean, we were telling the hairdresser "the Carrere Haircut" we want as we admired that blonde player who had the crowd growl with pleasure every time he had the ball. This crowd well dressed with their shoes shined, I found it again in 1966 during my first stay in England, when my host Mister Nicholls would take me to watch Tottenham Hotspurs games then lead by Jimmy Greaves the England hero of the only world cup England ever won. And I found also these wooden stands way much later in the Nadi and Nausori stadium in Fiji who reminded me the same stands of my childhood Lézignan stade du Moulin.

Rugby league was dominant at the time but could not be called Rugby for some political reasons inherited from the Vichy regime and so could be only called "Jeu à 13".

Lézignan was OUR team and of course we were at the grand final when they were France Champions for the first time at the Toulouse Stadium in 1961 beating Roanne 7-4, at the final whistle my father burst into an incontrollable joy, he could not stop repeating "Lézignan is Champion de France!" "Lézignan is Champion de France!" I had never seen my father so happy. Tears in his eyes he was hugging all of us and could not contain his joy. On the ride back, each time we were going through a village or a town, he would open the rooftop of the 403 Peugeot for us to stand up and wave our green and white flags and would honk till we reach the end of town.

My uncle unfortunately who used to work very long hours, on the passenger seat could not enjoy as much as he was tired with a headache.

During the game a supporter managed to bring inside the stadium his white horse that he had decorated with green paint. Once arrived in Lézignan, the borough was in total effervescence and the horse supporter had written the score on the horses butt, 7 on the left one, and 4 on the right one. Players finally arrived perched on the bus rooftop and got engulfed in the club headquarters that at the time was in a café just like most of the rugby clubs in France.

On that night we came back much later than usual and on the road back to Perpignan we could see the lighthouses along the coast that were blinking as few cars were on the road. I was not sleeping standing up in the back attentive on how my father was driving and switching gears, telling myself I could do the same.

My sister and brother would be fast asleep and my mother was telling me we could make out of me a lighthouse keeper, still I adored these night drives and did not miss a single minute of it till we arrived home and our dog Black that we would take with us of course would wake up as soon as we would approach the house and would dash out of the car with me to open the garage doors in which the Peugeot 403 would spend the night after this journey from Toulouse to Perpignan.

Lezignan 1961

Play with Your Heart

The cars were jostling on the road chocked by the heat and the crush. They barely move, despite the frightened looks of the drivers and passengers. Luggage spill over the roofs, they are poorly roped, stacked in a hurry. The buses are overcrowded; they spit the blackish air of their panicked lungs.

He looks for her in vain, may be in that bus, may be in this taxi where four women are squeezed and one of them could have been her. No one has time to answer him, to pay attention to his quest, he, the only white person in this herd of terrified people because all of the sudden hunt down.

His heart beats even faster, his shirt is soaked by the morning dampness that changes everything in the quiet town awaken brutally.

It is impossible to find her in this beginning of a disorganized escape. He abandons the chaos in which he was hoping to find a chance to see her and may be helping her.

He is back in the calm and silent house. The loud humming and the shouts make room to the discreet birds. In between the light curtains he meets the three women all excited by the perspective of such an enormity. He can smell the Parisian perfumes, their throats palpitate and they assail him with comments.

His wife is there, sitting and silent, she observes his anxiety and his annoyance about her girlfriends.

Her bright look floods the room of her intelligence, beautiful and distant at the same time. She knows about the dramas that do not need any words.

He leaves them to go freshen up, the shower tingles his eyes redden. The window offers the magnificent panorama that ignores the ugliness of the current drama. He sadly likes to admire the lagoon with its astonishing nuances of blue, the coconut tree branches that swing in the soft trade wind and the necklace of white waves on the coral reef.

A breathing makes him jump, he turns around and here she is, her big black eyes of a frightened doe implore him, he takes her in his arms and holds her tight. Her muscles do relax and her body abandons, she looks for his mouth that he cannot refuse her and her sighs of relief rise from her passionate body.

"I looked for you everywhere"

"I am hiding in your place"

"They must not find you here, you have to go"

"No I am scared, I don't want to leave you"

He looks at the door, the room, worried.

"Nobody knows I am here, take me..."

Her ebony body is already naked; he does not want to, he is scared to death. The women are downstairs and the military are going to carry out their threats.

But her passion has already taken in his sex the eyes closed. He does not want to push her back, to disappoint her. He can feel her desperation, her fear of the end.

She offers him her round butt. He takes her, his breath short, the head inebriated by the madness of the moment. He can feel her pleasure looking for eternity, his, who tries to escape a merciless confusion.

The embrace lasts, he almost wishes his wife comes and that all of this ceases and that her gleaming eyes find the solution to this instant of embarrassment and love.

She comes real strong. Her heat spreads in moans. He can see her beautiful body arch her muscles and it's finally over. He takes in his hands her face undone by the violence of the pleasure. Fear recedes little by little for more lucidity. Her smile lightens up gently, he has to think and act fast.

He showers her, dries her, she lets go like a child, he tells her to wait and lay down. She smiles again and closes her tired eyes.

Finally they are gone, outside no one could guess the drama. He fixes right in her eyes his wife who has already understood everything. She draws nearer and they embrace. Her body is his.

He explains her who is up there. Her beauty radiates even more when she sits down and takes him by the hand.

With her, hope is back.

The felt of the Embassy tries his best to calm the effervescence of the moment. The fax machine crackles non-stop, the agitated conversations are on the telephone, the grinder swallows frenetically the documents all of the sudden bulky.

No one adds the useless word, all engaged in a vital efficiency. The passports are here, documents for life, the only hope. He looks at the pile accumulating, his collaborators don't pay attention to him, he is lonely, stuck between these blue documents and the tainted glass window that reflect him back only a distant image and blurry of the horror that unfolds. He thinks about his duty, to international law, to his reserve requirement, to the foreign affairs school, to his ambitions as a diplomat, to the "realpolitik". He can still see the red ditch of massacred flesh, the one that the escort had hoped to hide from him.

The reports, the cables pile up and then the final words of this loyal informant mixed with the last instructions decoded hastily.

He opens the passports, faces who go by, who are waiting for him. He closes his eyes and jumps up when the secretary calls him. They are in the garden now. She is with them all.

The secretary reminds him about the official instructions. The helicopters will be here before dusk.

Take a decision.

He then thinks about the one who influenced him so much, the one who had prepared him so well for the combats of the game and of life. He recalls the dark space in which he had the last words of verity before shooting out in the light of the collective confrontation. He recalls his strong words coming out of his heart so they could all feel the courage and the intelligence of the fight.

He recalled his clear look and always teary at the moment of the beautiful victory.

He can still feel the embraces full of joy and sweat. He shivers with these righteous memories of a rugby player and man. He knows he can still count on him and on them.

His decision is taken, because he had told them before the game when they were all so scared:

"Play with you Heart"

Manon

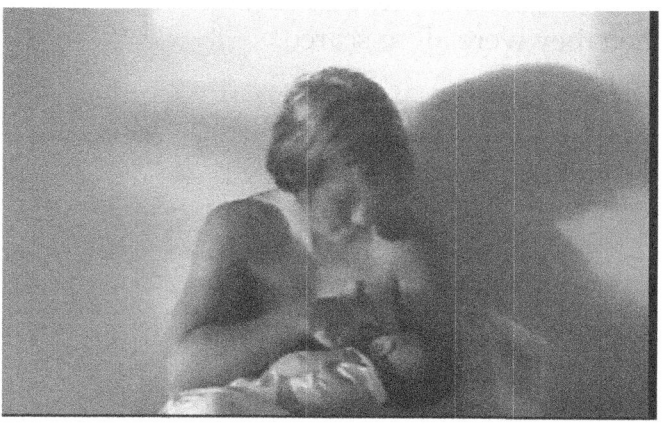

I was pacing around waiting for Maman to bring you into this world and finally a nurse with a smile in the corner of her lips and a very sweet voice came to get me to see you. She takes me to this door that opens on a dark room but just like a halo in a master's picture, a light brightened just you in the dark room, so as soon as I got into that room a dazzling of life brightens me, you turn right away towards me and look at me meaning to say "ah finally here you are", this look of love, with your pretty eyes, curious of the wait, engraves my head, my heart, my flesh, penetrates by all of my pores and gets settled in my soul for eternity.

This look that says, here I am Papa, I have been waiting for you for so long and yes here I am finally! My daughter. My love that I waited for, too.

The nurse can see me hesitating, stuttering, in this sublime moment, you are beautiful, as the caesarian babies are not deformed by the traumatizing mechanics of uterine birth. The nurse gently encourages me, seeing my shyness to take you into my arms, and I do I, the emotion is even stronger, it invades me and submerges me, I feel there when I hold you into my arms, this feeling that my philosophy professor had described that ultimate love is to be able to sacrifice your own life for a loved one, that this feeling you experience it so intensely for your own child, and yes indeed, it is there, this unconditional love, that love that can lead you to the ultimate sacrifice to give your own life. I don't want to let you go but Maman is waiting for me and I am worried about her, I delicately put you back, drop a kiss on your forefront fresh from your birth and I go to reassure Maman, who asks me right away on her bed "and the little one?" Yes I saw the little one, because she had not seen you yet…and I am unable to describe her this most beautiful moment of my life that I just had, just discovered, who is there in my moved heart and knocks me over each time I think about it. It fulfills my interior joy. I close my eyes and here again the magic moment, the moment that helps me survive, pass the life thunderstorms and tempest.

Suva 2000

Barefeet

Images of bare feet, beautiful images, graceful, free...

They are the young Melanesian girls in the street of Noumea they carry the shoes they took off in their hands. They walk bare feet, with suppleness and dignity in between sidewalks and lawns.

It's the lady in the shop window, she changes the clothing of the mannequin, she squats and her feet are bare feet. That was when I was small and that shop window fascinated me for the first time.

The lady is even more elegant and beautiful because she is bare feet; she has this erotic touch even if she wears transparent stockings.

It is She, with her small feet so petty that all other feet lose their charm compared to hers.

Bare feet, this is what my mother adored when as a child she would come holidaying in our village Gruissan. The first thing she was doing coming from the city was to go bare feet to wander from the garrigue to the lagoons.

The bare feet of Laisa the singer, she rehearses on the stage of the Travelodge hotel in Suva a Blues that makes her laugh in between two breaks.

Still more relaxed still more beautiful.

The Tahitian young woman, she climbs in the truck between Faa and Papeete. Reggae Music blasts out of the sound system. The warm and wet air rushes in through the open windows her bare feet brush me when she disembarks. She leans forward and her round boobs appear, the skin brown and smooth.

A beauty too furtive

Bare feet this is how my favorite rugby players do play. My little players from New Caledonia who invented the Kaneka rugby, here are the bare feet that sidestep and twirl for the joyous rugby.

"THEY WERE PLAYING BAREFEET!" exclaimed my uncle great sailor on the ocean liners when on port of call in the New Hebrides way before me. It is this image that he kept for the Port Vila rugby players.

Oh how ugly are those who spoil their bare feet in these American sandals with no grace, no aesthetic

A bare foot can barely stand a flip-flop and this one must be the thinnest to keep intact the erotic image of bare feet.

It is also this blonde young woman that I just glimpsed, she has blue light jeans, a very white t-shirt, her golden hair float into the wind, she is balancing herself on the edge of the sidewalk…bare feet…she has a clear smile.

The sensation under our feet of the wooden jetty heated by the sun, we wet it lightly with the salted lagoon water, and then the bare feet jump in the turquoise from the jetty, last sensation of an earthling to become fish or dolphin.

The woman is never as beautiful as when bare feet naked or not.

By the way in French, it should be written pieds nues

Nouméa 2008

Philosophy with Waisale Serevi

This is a philosophical interpretation of the famous Hong Kong Sevens try in 2007 in the semi final of the tournament versus New Zealand.

Viewing of the video clip:
http://www.youtube.com/watch?v=abY3U3hcQOU

We elaborated on this piece during a conference on leadership in the Pacific to illustrate the paper we presented about Waisale Serevi's leadership style. The conference took place at the University of the South Pacific in Suva, Fiji:
http://www.governance.usp.ac.fj/fileadmin/files/thematic/Leadership_Development/Case_Project/franck.pdf

COUNTER ATTACK

The video clip starts with a counter attack of the New Zealand team from inside their own 22 as Fiji is leading 15-12. A Fijian player, (Simione Saravanua), on the attack had lost the ball forward and Tomasi Cama the playmaker for New Zealand recovers the ball and launches the counter attack.

In rugby a ball won on a turn over is a perfect situation for counterattacking. In this situation the team who just lost the ball is defensively unorganized as they are in an attacking pattern. Teams who recover a ball in such a situation want to take advantage of this momentary state of disorganization in the defense by launching a counter attack that will exploit the open spaces in the disorganized defense.

This is exactly what New Zealand does and they run the ball on the near side of the field and almost the whole length until the Fijian player William Ryder inside the Fiji team own 22 meters finally catches one of their players.

GREAT LEADERS EMERGE IN CHAOTIC, DESPERATE SITUATIONS.

Historically and socially great leaders emerge in situation of chaos and desperation. It is in an environment where a group or a nation, seem to be in ultimate danger that the true leader will rise, come to the rescue, take charge and saves the group. This is exactly what Serevi will do in this situation. The situation at that point is desperate for the Fiji team, they cannot concede a try if not they lose the game; they are under tremendous pressure from New Zealand right inside their own 22 not far from their own goal line. Fiji needs a savior and this is when Serevi appears and takes charge.

Just like General De Gaulle took the leadership of the French resistance to the Nazis in the "second world war" as France was invaded and its Army on the run; just like Churchill delivered his speech of "Blood Sweat and Tears" as Britain was under the direct threat of Nazi invasion and rallied his people.

History and sociology recognize the great leaders in times of crisis.

AT THE RIGHT PLACE, AT THE RIGHT TIME.

In order to emerge as a savior, a leader, in a time of crisis or chaos, this person has to be at the right place, at the right time. De Gaulle was in London at the BBC to make his call to arms at the right time as France was diving into chaos under the Nazi's invasion. Churchill was prime minister of Great Britain just as the war seemed to be lost.

It is exactly where Serevi will be in this desperate game situation, right time and right place. He is perfectly positioned right behind the Fiji player, Cakau, who recovered the ball; he is standing in an open space and will calmly call for the pass even though the pressure from the opposition and the crowd screaming of excitement is enormous.

CALM, COMPOSED, CLEARHEADED

All great leaders don't panic under pressure but analyze the situation calmly and take the appropriate action. Great people, champions and leaders, do not take reckless decisions that could endanger the group; they will take calculated risks and in order to do so, they must first analyze and quickly decide. This is what Serevi does at that point. His vision of the field helps him in adapting instantly to the situation and in making the right decision.

ATTACK

Two New Zealand defenders are coming at him, but they are not exactly on the same line as a good defensive line should be. Serevi has space on both side of the field and on his right side he has one player, Simione Saravanua, in support, but Saravanua is wide and under the threat of the second defender.

So here we are in a situation of a 2 versus 2, but with space available. This situation calls for a counterattack ball in hand; kicking is not a good option as there are players in the deep end of the field to cover a possible kick. Kicking for touch is not part of the equation, as it would give the ball back to New Zealand with little time on the clock. In the crowd we hear: "go wide" which means to pass the ball wide to the support. (See Video clip filmed by spectators in the stands: http://www.youtube.com/watch?v=olaej5krE-g)

Instead Serevi runs towards the inside of defender 1 and as this defender follows his movement, Serevi will cut back outside with a devastating sidestep that will beat clearly defender 1. Serevi then straightens up as to take the gap and this motion attracts defender 2 towards his channel, another sharp sidestep will beat on the outside defender 2.

TAKE CHARGE

Serevi in just 2 quick steps and motions has turned the game around. From a desperate situation with his team on the back foot, now Fiji is going forward, Serevi is totally in charge, he is in control. "Follow me" now is the subliminal message to his teammates.

STEP OUT OF THE NORM

Another defender approaches with a good defensive angle from the inside but Serevi still has the support of the player Saravanua who just had to follow him. We have now the academic situation of 2 versus 1 that all good coaches teach first to their players. And what all coaches teach is to simply fix the defender in order to pass the ball to the unmarked player. What all players will do, that is fix and pass to the unmarked player, Serevi will not do. Just like when he got the ball and the crowd was yelling "out wide" and he did not. This is the trademark of the geniuses. Geniuses do not follow principles or methods or plans or don't do what is expected but adapt and create. In order to be a genius you have to go out of the mold, you cannot be just conventional.

So here we are with everyone expecting Serevi to pass the ball but he will not. Instead he will dummy the pass, the defender is fooled by the fake, jumps outside leaving his channel wide open for Serevi to run into.

Serevi is then out of the norm, of the conventional, surprises everyone and he gains at that point the status of greatness.

NOT A GAMBLE

Let's recall what we said earlier. Great people, leaders, do not take uncalculated risks, if Serevi fakes the pass to beat the defender it is because this defender in his run moved towards the outside shoulder of Serevi. An error that Serevi has detected and also provoked by running first to the outside then cutting back inside showing the ball all the way to distract the defender from Serevi footwork.

"AND WE PLAY"

In this action is shown the essence of what the game of rugby can be that is "play". Just like two children play to have fun, Serevi brings the fun, the joy of playing to solve problems. It is the illustration that, "play" in the total "ludic" sense, is the most powerful mean of approaching an issue and find a creative solution to it.

But in order to enjoy the game to the point of having the solutions come up instantly, the player must have complete freedom.

FREEDOM

Just like the writer, the poet, the artist, who creates a chef d'oeuvre, Serevi has total freedom to create and it is this freedom that enables him to be a genius of the game. It is also that freedom to improvise that forces the admiration of all. All admire him at that point not only for his physical and technical prowess but because he is a free man. The quest for Freedom is the one for all ordinary human beings and when one sees a free man it enhances in all of us the liberation of our spirit trapped in our social condition. Our heroes are free men and as this fantastic rugby phase of play is developed by Serevi, he becomes our hero, the one who has achieved what we are all looking for that is this ultimate liberty described by Philosopher Kant in a bird being able to fly as high as he likes.

RESERVE AND AVAILABILITY

Fiji plays against a formidable opponent and the retreating defense of New Zealand performs and traps Serevi and then tackles the Fijian player (Simione Saravanua) Serevi had to pass the ball to after he drew one more defender. This tackled player then passes the ball from the ground to another support player. Meanwhile Serevi is still playing. He plays without the ball in hand. He is in reserve of the action and as his teammates are in action he looks at the best way to beat the excellent defense.

Instead of keeping his position after passing the ball, he is still available for the game. He repositions himself by running outside the last ball carrier in the open space.

When one analyses the performance of a player, you will tend to look at the player only ball in hand or close to the action. As the play develops, the greatest players will "play without the ball" and work on finding the best position to be in, next. The hero disappears from the action but it is to reappear soon and conclude the epic story. The others are in the action; meanwhile he is in reserve of the next move, works hard and intelligently prepares his return, he is always available.

INVULNERABLE

It is thanks to his unnoticed work that Serevi gets the ball again, this time he is totally open, he runs towards the goal line, his run seems unstoppable, he runs on water, the goal line is closer. There is one defender coming across to catch him but he beats him yet with another inside cut and an incredible poise that reinforces the impression of invulnerability.

This last defender was desperate in his action, rushing to tackle him and looking so clumsy while Serevi was just gliding on the field, like an Albatross in the breeze leaving the common on the ground while he runs towards the glory of scoring.

HISTORY AND GREATNESS

The great don't just create history; they have the exceptional ability to mark history with a symbolic gesture. This is what Serevi does next.

As he runs towards the middle of the goal posts Serevi has this instant of genius that will mark history. He is running straight, the face full of joy and happiness, his body relaxed and he carries the ball high with the tips of his fingers. This image stays in history and translates the brilliance of the moment and of the man.

This gesture is a gesture full of meaning for the people of Rugby and the people of Fiji. It symbolizes the offering that Serevi makes to the Gods of rugby and its people. It is the ball that all of us dream to carry and cherish that he offers to all of us rugby lovers to see high and bright. It is the Holy Grail that he has won for us and brings back to us to admire and celebrate. Serevi knows at this instant that this could be his last try scored in the Hong Kong stadium the place where millions of fans have admired his rugby, and it is an "au revoir" that he means to give us in the most brilliant way. It is the conclusion not only of an absolute extraordinary play that will remain in all memories for eternity, but also the glorious end of a great rugby adventure. The gesture with his smile, wants to share his joy and his achievements with the public in the stadium all shouting and screaming of pleasure and accepting his offering.

This gesture is the Lion King presenting his son to his people on top of the mountain, it is De Gaulle with his arms extended way up to celebrate victory over the Nazis on the Paris balcony, it is Churchill with his V sign for victory, it is the GI's raising the flag on top of Iwo Jima.

This is how greatness is achieved not only by accomplishing a feat but also by seizing the moment with an inspiration that will engrave that moment.

SUPPORT

Serevi has his apostles with him in support. Right next to him even though there is just he and the goal line now. If the teammates are still in support it is because Serevi has always demanded from them to be there even if he is way in the clear. One day Serevi shared with us: "do you know why I did not score that many tries on the Irb circuit?... It is because I will often pass the ball to my support players to score instead of me, even when I am in the clear. This way I know they will still be in support the day I will need them."

This "confidence"/secret was a prophecy as Serevi is showing the ball to the people of Rugby his team-mates in immediate support warn him of an arriving threat in the form of Tomasi Cama who tries to take advantage of Serevi relaxed moment to catch him up. He then wisely chooses to tuck the ball against his body for a dive in the end zone, the Promised Land.

JUDAH

In order to understand the next episode we must go back in 2001 when Tomasi Cama senior was the 7's coach for Fiji. Even though Tomasi Cama was Waisale's team-mate back in the early 90's and scored that other memorable try for Fiji thanks to another incredible passage of play led by Serevi (http://www.youtube.com/watch?v=xU1o4U2jep4), Tomasi Cama would not select Serevi even though he was back then at the pinnacle of his career. It created enormous controversy in Fiji and many could not comprehend that Tomasi Cama the coach would not select Serevi in the Fiji team even though he was the best 7's player in the world. Many saw that as a betrayal.

Tomasi Cama's son plays for New Zealand and for some this is seen also as betraying his country of birth even though many admire his excellent play for New Zealand.

Given that background, with a father who would not select Serevi and playing for the enemy, Tomasi Cama jumps on Serevi on the ground way after he has landed after scoring. It is a blatant act of brutality that should warrant a yellow card. That act is to punish Serevi for his brilliance; it is to nail him on the ground like nailing him on the cross for being so holy. Who else can do that but a "Judah" and that moment is another extraordinary symbolic gesture of our poor human nature. It is the sign that us humans can be the carriers of pettiness and cruelty. This is when the apostles come to the rescue; Naevo and Vucago confront Cama but too late. Just like the Albatross in the Baudelaire poem, Serevi has been brought down to the mediocrity of human nature and his majesty while gliding in the sky turned into clumsiness when on the ground.

Often, to amuse themselves the men of the crew
Lay hold of the albatross, vast birds of the seas
Who follow, sluggish companions of the voyage
The ship gliding on the bitter gulfs.

Hardly have they placed them on the planks,
Than these kings of the azure, clumsy and shameful,
Let, piteously, their great wings in white,
Like oars, drag at their sides.

This winged traveler, how he is awkward and weak!
He, lately so handsome, how comic he is and uncomely!
Someone bothers his beak with a short pipe,
Another imitates, limping, the ill thing that flew!

The poet resembles the prince of the clouds
Who is friendly to the tempest and laughs at the bowman;
Banished to ground in the midst of hootings,
His wings, those of a giant, hinder him from walking.

- Charles Baudelaire

It is with this poem that we will conclude our essay on philosophy with Serevi as it illustrates so well Serevi's fate in his country. He is not a prophet in his country and too many driven by the mediocrity of their soul behave as the sailors in Baudelaire poem towards "the prince of the clouds". Those who could not achieve the freedom we humans are ultimately seeking will not want to let the other enjoy it.

Fiji Olympic Champion

During our interview to recruit the new Coach for Fiji, Ben Ryan had the largest smile, kindness and a touching modesty, but most of all he knew the Fijian game better than any other candidate and even better than the Fijian candidates themselves.

It is in this smile that illustrates the joy of sharing the "joie de vivre", the enjoyment of life that you will find one of the main reasons of the Fijian triumph.

So he was the first choice without a doubt, in spite of the reservations from some (…)

Fiji is the only nation who really has selected its best players for the Olympic games because the Fijian rugby players are the Fijian people's players; they are not the egocentric club president's players. They are our friends, our cousins, our brothers, our sons, our Vanua (our land).

Their values are those who seduce all those who approach the Fijian players, Humility, Tradition, Respect that give to Fijian Rugby its strong identity.

May many in the World find these values rooted in your regional identities, with your own language, dances and songs; this is the lesson hopefully Fijian rugby has given. Without a strong identity and its rituals a team cannot be as irresistible as Fiji Sevens.

But mainly may all let the children play! The Rugby from Fiji who has triumphed is the one who plays, who is joyous around 4 pm in all fields, streets and schoolyards that you can find at that magic hour all over Fiji. This is the magician's secret, rugby is played with touch rugby in order to laugh, to enjoy and all the coaches around the globe must understand that play is not something that you learn but something that you celebrate through enjoyment and fun.

The Fijian kids, future Olympic champions have learned rugby in the enjoyment of the game of touch rugby, the fun of it, the free game advocated by Pierre Villepreux. This game of freedom generates free skills that are the matrix of the creativity, of the magic that commentators like to mention to brand the Fijian game.

Coach Ben Ryan's genius was to make sure that the players had spaces of freedom when ball in hand and he put in place thoroughness in the basics such as set pieces, defense and the contact areas where the warrior's spirit of the Fijian players found its outlet.

The athleticism of the players did the rest, Fijian other than their speed have very large hands and exceptional arm's span that allow them to catch and pass the ball in the most acrobatic ways. The Olympic champions grew up bare feet and that explains the incredible footwork that confuses the defenders.

Then the Fijian game plays itself with a terrific efficiency because it is adapted to the particular talents of the players. Fiji has the best strike rate of all teams and needs only short plays to score because the ball does not go to ground for a breakdown, Fiji is the team who rucks the least and makes full sense of our philosophy of play that considers rucks as just "accidents of the game".

This style of play was endangered of disappearing in the first decade of this century because of the influence of foreign coaches and also because players moving overseas were losing their identity. We reintroduced it with the Nadroga Province as early as 2010 first with the under 20 team then the following year with the seniors and since then the main province of Fiji rugby who provides the majority of the star Fiji rugby players across the world, has reigned on the archipelago's rugby with absolute domination and has our supporters dance with joy and excitement.

But this unique capacity to keep the ball alive is to be found in the development of the players through the "freedom game" that is touch rugby. Touch rugby is played everywhere in the world but in Fiji the rules are special and I never played these rules anywhere but in Fiji. Everywhere on the rugby planet, the ball is turned over after 3 or 4 or sometimes more "touch". Not in Fiji, in Fiji the ball is turned over after the first touch with one hand only. This detail has a crucial and decisive importance in the development of the player. When all the players around the globe are initiated to the game by playing touch "3 or 4 touch" or by tackle rugby, these players are reassured in their decision making because if they are touched or tackled, the possession of the ball is not lost and the player has not done a serious mistake; he will be able to play with the ball again. That is not the case in Fiji with touch rugby one hand/one touch because when the player is touched he committed a serious mistake because the ball is turned over. Therefore this player will have to be much more alert in his decision making, he will have to gather quickly information, his field of vision will have to be the widest possible, he must know where the defenders are, where his support players are and he will have to develop very diverse strategic skills in order to avoid at all cost the opponent; inside cuts, change of pace, fakes, acrobatic passes, its all good to avoid at all cost to be touched. Touch rugby Fijian rules is much more demanding than any other form of touch rugby around the world; it forces the player to learn how to release the ball before contact and all at the same time fix the defender. It forces the player to anticipate much quicker than players initiated to the game through the game of 3 touch or more, or initiated through tackle rugby as the rules of rugby favor the player going to ground and therefore reassures the player in not taking risky decisions. So this player's development, done "naturally" makes the Fijian player way superior in his spatiotemporal perception in order to keep the ball alive who by its constant movement will disorganize the defenses.

We have also the notion of sharing the ball, sharing the pleasure to pass it and offer it to another. There is a ritual in touch rugby in Fiji that whoever you are, beginner, tourist, experienced player as soon as you join a game the ball will be passed to you. Its like an offering, an invitation to the joy of the game but its also a ritual who translates a will not to be selfish while playing by keeping the ball but instead sharing it with his/her partners.

That's how touch rugby Fijian style played daily by all kids and adults is a key factor in the triumph of Fijian rugby at the Olympic games.

Religion plays also a dominant role in this triumph because it brings in the mental preparation that all the sport psychologists recommend for high performance. It brings serenity before the game and return to a state of calm after the game. The pre-match rituals such as praying and hymns help the players in their pre-match routine that is necessary for high performance. This religious routine allows lucidity and a courage that the elite athletes need before a game.

Finally how can we forget this nation crazy of its rugby who screams and laughs in the stadium, is entertained easily and jumps and dances of joy even when the opposite team scores! For those who like myself have played and coached in front of belligerent crowds and under despicable invectives on the French or American rugby grounds; it is so refreshing, it is so pleasant and such an honor to coach and participate in THE Rugby country.

Let the children play, burst into laughter instead of whining and complaining respect each person and go back to your culture and its rituals, dances, songs and then the rugby will become as beautiful as it was in the final of the Rio Olympic games.

The Last Men, the Real Ones

We are on the mountain plateau of Navosa, situated in the heart of Viti Levu, the main islands of the Fiji Archipelago.

The rugby players came down from the hills and valleys around, riding their horses and are going to battle with those coming from the coral coast. These last ones left early the blue lagoons and the white foams of the Pacific Ocean that break on the reef, to come up the Sigatoka river in wind broken lorries on a dirt dusty road. Today's event is the selection of the Navosa Rugby team, a proud Fiji Province.

The ones from the mountains are not going to be a match for the ones from the coast. Not because they are not as strong and agile, but because the inhabitants from the highlands are traditionally mainly gardeners when the ones from the coast are traditionally warriors. These warriors had the task to repel the waves of invaders coming from Tonga. The difference is striking in the rugby game when the dire descendants of these fighters have an exceptional aptitude for this game of collective combat. The Navosa province then will have a majority of players selected from the coast, where are found the warriors who protect the country.

This is how the best Fiji rugby players come from this coastal region that includes the province of Nadroga and Navosa.

Virtually most of the players who are in the European professional championships are from that region of warrior's tradition.

In the Fiji society, the warrior status is the most prestigious one. More than the priest, the doctor or the fisherman, it sparks admiration and respect. The supreme honor for a young Fijian man is to be this warrior; it will be the same in Tonga and Samoa

Ever since the missionaries arrived, there are no more tribal wars but the ancestral spirit remains. In their luggage the missionaries also brought rugby who is going to substitute irresistibly the war tradition. So the young Oceania men from proud warriors are going to transform themselves in formidable rugby players and in the collective conscience of the Oceania islands people is going to replace this fundamental axis that defines the Fijian, Tongan and Samoan societies: the warrior tradition.

The Tongan teams are called Tautahi (warriors); the Fijian teams are called warriors or Bati (warrior in Fijian).

Everything in the rugby representation refers to the warrior spirit with the journalistic expressions, the traditional and cultural ceremonies and of course, the teams who challenge the opposition with the pre game war dances, the "Cibi" for the Fiji, the "Siva" for Samoa and the "Sipi Tau" for Tonga all are dances/chants calls for the combat.

These traditions don't go without social and political consequences in these countries.

Fiji has an army who is the pride of the country. As the soldier (modern warrior) is admired, feared, honored.

When the commodore Vorege Bainimarama head of the armies and president of the Fiji Rugby Union, stages a coup the Fijian people offers little resistance.

The Warrior is a source of income for Fiji. Its soldiers are immensely appreciated by the United Nations who deploys them all over the world as blue helmets. Their courage, discipline, composure and imposing physique gave them a great reputation. There are stories in Iraq that in situations where American soldiers would not get into, Fijians would.

In Iraq and its region, security private firms recruit Fijians who are no longer in the army. Salaries of these dangerous jobs are more than attractive for Fijian apt to combat.

Then British, French, Australian, Japanese and New Zealander clubs buy another category of Fijian warriors, the rugby players whose talent is sought after.

In fact each of the National teams from these countries would have a Fijian born player in its ranks.

This massive migration of Fijian men brings to the country significant remittances with the women taking more and more importance in the management of the domestic economy.

We are now in a block of a ghetto area near San Francisco, East Palo Alto, who in the middle of the 90's is abandoned by the authorities to the violent gangs, drug dealers and other criminals. This big block of houses is the Tongan one with Tongans who migrated to California. In this perimeter, no crime, no dealers, everyone stays away from the Tongans who have the reputation to fight like no one. The Tongan players that we coach take us there without issue and no one would even dare to attack.

Chris one of our few Afro-American player we coach open his eyes wide open just by mentioning the word Tongan.

This incredible ferocity in the combat is the Tongan culture and draws its source from the saying: "the Tongan mountain is his heart. When you use that spirit, no mountain is high enough, nor difficult or insurmountable ". The Tongan draw that ferocity in combat to an infallible faith in their invincibility.

Each island group in Tonga had specialized warriors. Those from Tongatapu were land warriors, those from Haapai were redoubtable sailors marauders, and the ones from Va'vau were both.

The ancestors were the lords of the Pacific Ocean navigating on immense distances for warfare and conquer new islands.

The descendants are also in great numbers emigrants now in New Zealand, Australia, California, and Hawaii and bring with them this reputation of big fighters.

However Tongans are extremely kind by nature and have the best sense of humor in the Pacific. But beware of an angry Tongan ready to fight.

They too have exported hundreds of rugby players all over the globe with the most famous one Jonah Lomu.

Anthropologists explain that with the very long voyages on canoes done by the elders, only the biggest people could resist to the cold because the largest is the skin surface for men, the bigger is his resistance to hypothermia. This natural selection makes Tongans the most massive people in the world by its size. Other than these exceptional measurements that makes them the strongest people, the rugby Tongan players like to consider themselves as the direct descendants of the great warriors. The Tautahi reds selection once surprised everyone by winning once the Pacific Championship. But what was not a surprise was that this team was formed mainly of players from the village of Ha'ateiho who is the village of the great Tonga chief Tu'I Ha'ateito himself direct descendant of Tamaha, the holy Daughter who has the highest ranking, even higher than the king of Tonga. The best warriors for her protection always surrounded Tamaha. They were thoroughly selected in the Tamaha parenthood and the village of Ha'ateiho always had this warrior's tradition. They were the fiercest of the old times and modern times. Still today this village is feared and respected. Its members are invincible thanks to their strength and tenacity. A Tongan warrior will fight till death if necessary, and that explains how much were they feared in this dangerous area of East Palo Alto.

The local rugby team of Samoa, looks small in size.

All the big and hefty ones play their rugby overseas and are the best in the World such as the Tuilagi brothers.

In spite of their small size, the team won that year, the pacific tournament. The reason being: the discipline and extraordinary homogeneity of the team that reflects well the one of the country.

In Samoa, the warrior is not a specificity; each and everyone must be a warrior, gardener, or fisherman at a time. A social order is in place, based on the pride of the people and its total commitment. If in Fiji, there are tensions, (positive or negative) with the soldiers warriors, in Tonga a war violence sometimes not well channeled, in Samoa, the social integration of the warrior role defines an exceptional esprit de corps.

The Samoan rugby player's performance finds its source in the absolute confidence of the social order. Each and everyone have his place and role well defined just like in the village where the Matai is the noble that leads.

The song Manu Samoa by the band Te Vaka

> *Aiu Manu Samoa*
> *Aiu ma le aloa iai*
>
> *Aiu manu Samoa*
> *Tama tamatoa e toa lama*
>
>
> *Go Manu Samoa*
> *Go with all your strength*
>
> *Go Manu Samoa*
> *Our men, our warriors*

The definition is clear for the Samoans; the rugby players are our men, our warriors.

A Samoan warrior is more a servant than an aggressor; the warrior's role is first to serve the one he represents. But these warriors are also the ones who are the more capable to serve, they are experts in their art as defenders of those that he represents. They also represent the "mana" or the integrity of the People they serve. So is the definition of a rugby player according to the Samoan terms. The players are seen not only like the representative of the people but also the people's honor. They are also considered as expert in their art (rugby) and as such they are representing their people but also are the defenders of their people through rugby.

Here are three proud people like no other, three rugby nations like no other. The Tongan, Fijian and Samoan are more than rugby players, they carry a tradition.

A tradition where they all sing beautifully, and all dance perfectly.

The game of war, dance, singing, here are the last men, the real ones.

Thanks to my rugby players

Mesui and Solo Taufeulungaki (Tonga)

Alfred Shuster (Samoa)

Pichou

When I first arrived in this beautiful villa, I had not gone far from my litter…I could still feel their presence and I was not scared as right away I felt love in this new home of mine. There were two adorable little girls and one of them was officially my mom, when the other one so adorable as well had a very kind pet dog called Princesse. There was also another big brother called Mickey. Me I was given the name Pichou as I was so small and the monsieur of the house called me that way in his Provençal language in which he would call me up at times.

I grew quickly as I was so well fed and most of all cajoled, then my little mistresses quickly seduced me by cuddling me and feeding me well and also by having me do jumping exercises that were filling them with joy when I was being so obedient.

There was also this large green space at the back of the villa in which my big sister and I would run madly. One day I had the scare of my life, a huge lightning with a terrifying noise fell on that green space where I was going about, then I think I never run as fast as I did ever in my life and that made my big master laugh a lot.

Another time, my little mistresses had firecrackers explode all around the villa. This time too, I was scared to death and escaped the home and my big master found me only the next day after that terrifying evening.

There was also in this family, this lady with clear eyes who was always worried about me but was always pampering me especially when I was sick. But one day as she was driving out of the garage where I was fast asleep, she drove over my hip and my grand mistress was catastrophic because I could not walk any longer. So my big master took me to these veterinarians who wanted to insert a pin in my hip and send me to Australia for surgery because they did not know I was a real Fijian and I healed all by myself after a little while. My big master filmed me running around and went to show it to these veterinarians who got vexed.

I was a good guard for the house with my big sister Princesse. But I was mad with myself not to protect my beautiful now grown up mistress when thieves that I would have loved to bite down attacked her inside the house.

I adored the long walks on the beach and the ones we were doing in the forest to reach fresh cascades where our pretty mistresses would take us now that they knew how to drive.

I adored also to "fish" and would stay for hours in the clear water watching fish and trying to catch any, which I never did…I would jump feet together in the water to no avail.

Then one day arrived a new little sister, adopted by my little mistress. I must admit I was a little jealous, but in the end she was real nice and it made my little mistress so happy and that's all that mattered to me.

I adored also climbing in the cars, and feeling the fresh air caress my muzzle, my head outside the window…

Then my big brother left discreetly in his sleep.

Then it was my big sister turn and I felt an immense despair because my big sister was so kind even thought she would bark at this poor man who was coming clean the pool each morning.

My health got worse, and my beautiful big mistress would look after me even more with all sorts of medicine but I still loved to scamper around and follow my two kindest mistresses who were more like my big sisters.

Little by little my sight got worse until I could no longer see the beautiful colors of the island where I was born. But my strong spirit helped me overcome this handicap and I was always able to find my way back thanks to my exceptional flair.

Then things degraded for me but at least I could feel the love of my big master who kept on taking me to long walks that I really needed so that I would not be bored and I had new companions full of energy who encouraged me to come over and frolic with them and were crying of joy each time we would leave for walks. Then my little mistresses now grown up left on the other side of the ocean and I did not feel them that much any longer but my two big masters were still around even though they sometimes would be away for weeks and it was this lady that my big master called Milikator who would look after us even though she could not pronounce my name properly and called me Pijou at dinner time.

My grand master love I felt it even more when I was so sick that each day he would bath me in the sea to relieve my pains, he would bath me twice and massage me in the water all the while encouraging me, then came the last bath before my big departure.

Where I am now I do not suffer any longer but I miss the birds who sing happily in the mornings that shine of a thousand bright colors, I will also miss the cricket's whispers who rocked me at night under the starry skies, the joyful shouts of happiness from my mistresses jumping in the pool, the garden multicolored flowers, the calls of the pigeon in the forest, the parrots gliding, the kula who squeals in their dazzling flights, the king fisher who is the last one to go asleep and say good bye to the sun already down in the orange and red horizon of a clear day.

Thank you my family for such a beautiful life.

Afterword

All of these writing would have not been incepted without a turn in life that changes a destiny.

There are some people in your life who influence it more than any, Stanley Shure and Gary Cardiff, showed up in my club Perpignan and we became quickly best friends as I was the only one speaking English in the team. Quickly Stan became a warrior like my Catalan people adore, he was fearsome, making huge  tackle from his American football background that at the time we did not know about. In a game versus Beziers our archrivals of the time this infamous lock called Alain Esteve who was feared on all rugby grounds in France was lined up against us, he was a huge guy and his dirty game was as huge as his size, our forwards were definitely intimidated, but for Stan, it was Alain who?

So he took that guy head on hitting him left and right, knocking him on the ground, so our teammates were going what? If this guy can do it, we can do it and the big dirty lock was no longer untouchable and had probably the worst afternoon of his rugby career. After this Stan became a legend in my club USAPerpignan. His fierce and physical attitude never saying die was an inspiration for all. But now here we are in Toulon. Playing again against the toughest and dirtiest team of the time. Playing away in France, means you are in adversary territory and usually you take a low profile, but not Stan who did not know any better and all hell broke loose, us Catalans, are descendants of mercenaries and there were fights all over the ground as we were beating Toulon all over the park. At one point there was this infamous prop called Baldaccino who had stuck Stan on the ground and hitting his face repeatedly I was about to go kick that guy in the face when the ball popped out of the ruck and I had to go tackle that center to fill my defensive duty. Eventually we lost the game by three points but not the fight...

At the end of the season Stan and Gary asked me if I would like to go coach their team as I had passed all my coaching diplomas on top of my MA in political sciences. I said yes sure and then did not think much about it, but in the middle of the summer I received this green letter with green stationary from Tony Scott then president of the team inviting me to take the position of Head Coach I supposed on Stan's strong recommendation.

So in October 1980 I took a laker skytrain from London at a ridiculous price and when I landed in Los Angeles, here was Stan greeting me with a "welcome to Los Angeles!" We used to practice at night in La Valley college who was a nice venue but on the other side of the hill from where Stan was living with his parents, and each night after training we would stop at this burger joint where the guy would call our number even though we were the only clients late at night (gee these Americans are strange I was saying to myself), to make the story shorter at the post game party vs. the Grunions that we had destroyed by a large score, I was introduced by Bill Broz to Elise and that was the start of a great adventure.

Thanks to Stan, this is where I started my rugby coaching career at the age of 28, with Eagle Rock AC, who took me to the USA women's eagles, Stanford university with the only win versus Cal in the big game in 43 years and 3 appearances in final 4. Thanks to Eagle Rock and Manasa Baravilala after a stay at Grammar Auckland, Elise and I ended up in Fiji where I got to prepare the National team in 1988 for their successful Europe tour where they beat the French barbarians with Naas Botha at 10, then I landed the job at the University of the South Pacific for 5 years followed by FRU who recruited me as their coaching director, all of this thanks to Stan who passed away on June 18 2023 after a tough fight who he only, could fight...but his suffering was so unbearable that he asked for it to be over. He has charmed my daughters with his kindness and support, always welcoming them in his Los Angeles home, he had a great sense of humor, a sharp mind, composed always, I was lucky enough in 2021 to spend time with him on an extended stopover that I really enjoyed in his company, I had brought him a USAPerpignan Jersey, he was a clearheaded smart lawyer I understand.

Here you are Stan up in the sky, next time I see you I will pass you the ball for one more try up there in heaven where I don't belong...

Thank you to former Stanford players Jeff Freund and Timur Yarnall for support in editing and publishing this collection.

And, of course, to Elise, without whom most stories would have not been told.

About the Author

Franck Boivert was born in 1952 in Perpignan, France.

He graduated from the Institut de Sciences poliques Aix en Provence International relations

- Head coach for Eagle Rock rugby club Los Angeles
- Head coach UCLA men and women
- Coach/player Gentlemen of Aspen
- Head Coach Bats of San Francisco
- Head Coach Pacific Coast Grizzlies women
- Head Coach Stanford University men and women
- Head Coach USA National women's team
- Director of the University of the South Pacific rugby program
- Coaching Director Fiji rugby Union
- Head Coach Tahiti National 7's team

- Trainer International Rugby Board
- Coaching Director Nadroga Rugby union
- Author of the Rugby Manual for the South Pacific, published by The University of the South Pacific

Made in United States
Orlando, FL
24 March 2024